Spiritual Reality
or
Obsession

D0062477

WATCHMAN NEE

Translated from the Chinese

Christian Fellowship Publishers, Inc.
New York

Available from the Publishers at:
11515 Allecingie Parkway
Richmond, Virginia 23235

PRINTED IN U.S.A.

TRANSLATOR'S PREFACE

Christians today are seeking for reality. In the present book, Watchman Nee illustrates with practical instances how every spiritual thing has its reality. This reality is in the Holy Spirit, and the Holy Spirit alone leads us into reality. He further warns believers against a common ill, which is obsession, by pointing out its symptoms and causes and also the way of deliverance.

CONTENTS

Translator's Preface   1

1. Spiritual Reality: What It Is   5

2. Spiritual Reality: Its Relationships   27

3. Spiritual Reality: How to Enter In   39

4. Obsession: What It Is   47

5. Obsession: Causes and Deliverance   57

chapter 1

spiritual reality:
what it is

God is a Spirit: and they that worship him must worship in spirit and truth. (John 4.24)

Howbeit when he, the Spirit of truth, is come, he shall guide you into all the truth. (John 16.13)

And it is the Spirit that beareth witness, because the Spirit is the truth. (1 John 5.7)

One thing which God's people should take note of is that every spiritual matter has its reality before God. If what we have touched is mere appearance and not reality, we shall find that it is of no spiritual value whatsoever. What, then, is spiritual reality? The reality of a spiritual thing is something spiritual, not material. Although spiritual reality is often expressed in words, those words, however many, are not the reality. Although spiritual reality needs to be disclosed in our lives, the set formalities of our lives are not reality. Although spiritual reality must be manifested in conduct, human-manufactured pretension is not reality.

What is spiritual reality? "God is a Spirit: and they that worship him," says the Lord, "must worship in spirit and truth." The word "truth" means "trueness" or "reality." The same applies to the following words: "Howbeit, when he, the Spirit of truth, is come, he shall guide you into all the truth." "And it is the Spirit that beareth witness, because the Spirit is the truth." These all reveal that God is Spirit, therefore all that is related to God is in the Spirit. The Spirit of truth is the Spirit of reality. For this reason, spiritual reality must be in the Spirit. It is that which transcends man and matter. Only what is in the Holy Spirit is spiritually real, because all spiritual things are nurtured in the Holy Spirit. Once anything is outside the Holy Spirit, it turns into letters and forms which are dead. Spiritual things are real, living, and full of life only when they are in the Holy Spirit. It is the Holy Spirit who guides us into all reality. Whatever may be entered into without the guidance of the Holy Spirit is definitely not spiritual reality. All which one can obtain merely by listening or thinking or being emotionally involved is not spiritually real. We must remember that the Holy Spirit is the executor of all spiritual matters. What God does today is done in the Holy Spirit. Only what the Holy Spirit does is truly real.

Whatever is in the Holy Spirit is real. If anyone touches this reality he obtains life, for life and reality are joined together. Whoever desires to attend to spiritual life must stress spiritual reality. The one who has touched spiritual reality in the Holy Spirit will immediately respond with an amen in his heart whensoever he meets another who has also touched spiritual reality—and vice versa. This is what is meant by the words in Psalm 42.7, "Deep calleth unto deep." It can be said that reality touches reality. For a better understanding, let us now illustrate with some concrete instances.

INSTANCE 1

"Jesus answered, Verily, verily, I say unto thee, Except one be born of water and the Spirit, he cannot enter into the kingdom of God" (John 3.5). This is the word of our Lord to Nicodemus.

When Paul wrote to the saints in Rome he inquired, "Are ye ignorant that all we who were baptized into Christ Jesus were baptized into his death?" Paul then continued with these words: "We were buried therefore with him through baptism into death: that like as Christ was raised from the dead through the glory of the Father, so we also might walk in newness of life. For if we have become united with him in the likeness of his death, we shall be also in the likeness of his resurrection" (Rom. 6.3-5). Both the Lord Jesus and Paul speak of the reality of baptism.

But some people look at this matter of baptism from the physical point of view. Their eyes see only the water. Hence they insist on baptismal regeneration. They have not touched the spiritual reality. Other people try to approach this question mentally. They maintain that water cannot regenerate people. Accordingly, they explain that with some people baptism is real and inward while with others it is false and outward. The first group can enter into the kingdom of God, but those in the second category are excluded. They too have not touched spiritual reality in this matter.

The baptism of which the Lord told Nicodemus is a reality. Paul also sees reality in baptism: burial with the Lord for newness of life. He told the saints in Colossae, "Having been buried with him in baptism, wherein ye were also raised with him" (Col. 2.12). To him baptism and burial are one and the same thing; so too are baptism and resurrection. He knows what is meant by being buried with the Lord and also what is meant by being raised with the Lord. He does not see the water of baptism only, nor does he view some as being truly baptized while some others are not. He communicates to others the reality of that baptism which he has touched.

Brothers and sisters, if you have seen baptism as a reality you naturally know what it is. The question of its being true or false, inward or outward, simply does not exist, because you see that to be baptized is to be buried and raised up together with Christ. Having seen this reality, can you refrain from proclaiming that baptism is indeed so big, so real, and so inclusive? As soon as a person is shown the reality, then that which is false can no longer exist. Suppose someone should say: "Now that I have been baptized, I hope I may be buried and then raised together with the Lord." The one who could utter such a statement has not touched reality, since to him baptism is one thing and burial and resurrection are quite another. But that person who perceives spiritual reality knows what burial and resurrection are. Baptism is burial, baptism is also resurrection. They are one and the same thing.

Do you realize, brothers and sisters, that no one can ever perceive spiritual things with his eyes fixed on the material, that no one can ever think through to the spiritual with his brain? All spiritual matters have their realities. He who has touched reality questions no more.

INSTANCE 2

The same is true with the breaking of bread. On the night of His betrayal the Lord Jesus "took bread, and blessed, and brake it; and he gave to the disciples, and said, Take, eat, this is my body. And he took a cup, and gave thanks, and gave to them, saying, Drink ye all of it, for this is my blood of the covenant, which is poured out for many unto remission of sins. But I say unto you, I shall not drink henceforth of this fruit of the vine. . . ." (Matt. 26.26-29). Some view this from the physical standpoint, and hence they maintain that as the bread and the cup are being blessed the whole substance of the bread is converted into the body of the Lord and the whole substance of the fruit of the vine is changed into the blood of the Lord. Others view it from the rational approach, arguing that the bread and the wine have not been transubstantiated (as in the above case) but that they merely represent the body and the blood of the Lord.

Judging from the Lord's own word, however, we see that He lays emphasis neither on transubstantiation nor on representation but on spiritual reality. Behind that which is eaten and drunk is the spiritual reality. Jesus says "this is my body"; He does not say "this represents my body." And after He says "this is my blood of the covenant" the Lord continues with, "I shall not drink henceforth of this fruit of the vine"—clearly indicating that the wine has neither been transubstantiated nor is representative of the blood. When the Lord speaks of the bread and of the cup, His whole emphasis is on that reality. In His eyes there is neither representation nor transubstantiation.

Paul articulates the same thing when he declares, "The cup of blessing which we bless, is it not a communion of the blood of Christ? The bread which we break, is it not a communion of the body of Christ?" (1 Cor. 10.16) It is the bread, yet he acknowledges it as the body of Christ. It is the cup, yet he accepts it as the blood of Christ. In Paul's eyes, there is neither representation nor transubstantiation, only spiritual reality. He further explains: "seeing that we being many, are one loaf, one body" (v.17 Darby). How could he say this unless he has touched spiritual reality?

When a person speaks, he utters either a fact or a parable—that which is couched in literal or in symbolic language. This is not so with Paul. "We who are many" is literal; "are one loaf" is symbolical. He joins the literal and the symbolic in one sentence because to him both "we being many" and "are one loaf" are facts. The spiritual reality which he has touched is so factual that he is able to unite "we being many" with "are one loaf, one body." He has transcended grammar and rhetoric. Here is one who really knows the Lord. When he takes up the bread he is truly in communion with the body of Christ, for he has forgotten the bread and is now in touch with the spiritual reality. When he takes up the cup he is indeed in communion with the blood of Christ, for he has forgotten the fruit of the vine and has touched the spiritual reality. Having touched spiritual reality, for him word or doctrine presents no problem.

INSTANCE 3

As to the matter of the church, it is really something marvelous to behold. Some people think there are true churches and false churches. But the Lord says to Peter:

> *And I also say unto thee, that thou art Peter, and upon this rock I will build my church; and the*

> *gates of Hades shall not prevail against it. I will*
> *give unto thee the keys of the kingdom of heaven:*
> *and whatsoever thou shalt bind on earth shall be*
> *bound in heaven; and whatsoever thou shalt loose*
> *on earth shall be loosed in heaven. (Matt.*
> *16.18-19)*

This is what the church is in the Lord's thought. The church in His mind is nothing but the true one. This applies not only to the church universal but likewise to the church local. Explains the Lord further:

> *If thy brother sin against thee, go, show him his*
> *fault between thee and him alone: if he hear thee,*
> *thou hast gained thy brother. But if he hear thee*
> *not, take with thee one or two more, that at the*
> *mouth of two witnesses or three every word may*
> *be established. And if he refuse to hear them, tell*
> *it unto the church: and if he refuse to hear the*
> *church also, let him be unto thee as the Gentile*
> *and the publican. Verily I say unto you, What*
> *things soever ye shall bind on earth shall be bound*
> *in heaven; and what things soever ye shall loose on*
> *earth shall be loosed in heaven. (Matt. 18.15-18)*

According to the Lord, when the church declares a brother to be right, he is most assuredly right, and when the church pronounces him to be wrong, he is undeniably wrong. As we read this, a question easily comes to our mind: What if the decision of the church is faulty? The Lord, nonetheless, speaks of the *reality* of the church. A wrong decision cannot come from what is real, since an incorrect decision will not be of the Holy Spirit but will be of the will of man. The church in the eyes of the Lord is a reality; whatever is outside that reality has absolutely no place in our Lord's thought.

When Paul mentions the church in his epistles, he speaks of it as the called, the sanctified, and a habitation of God (Rom. 1.7; 1 Cor. 1.2; Eph. 2.22).

The Apostle John speaks of the church in the same way as Paul. Though the seven churches in Asia have many faults and failures, nonetheless John still calls them the churches. Even the Lord Jesus acknowledges that "the seven candlesticks are seven churches" (Rev. 1.20).

To the apostles the church is a reality; there is therefore no problem of a false church in their eyes. This is not to imply that in the world there are no false churches. It only bespeaks the fact that he who fails to see the reality of the church is faulty in his sight. He who regards appearance takes all the churches as true. He who judges rationally finds some to be true and others false. Only in the eyes of the one who has touched the spiritual reality is the church spiritual beyond question.

Let us mention one point on the practical side. We may ask what body life is. Body life is not brought in by acting in accordance with a certain procedure. Only when you have touched spiritual reality can you touch the church; and then your actions become movements in the body rather than their standing as independent activities. For example, when you are about to take some action, it is not because you have fulfilled a required procedure—in inviting all the brothers and sisters to come and in consulting with them—that your action can be reckoned as body life. You are living out body life only when you have touched its reality while fellowshiping with brothers and sisters (whether many or few). If you have not contacted spiritual reality, then what is agreed upon unanimously by the whole assembly is only the opinion of the flesh. It is not in the least body life. Body life flows out of spiritual reality.

The case in Acts 15 demonstrates to us what body life is. For the purpose of solving the problem as to whether Gentiles must be circumcised, the apostles and elders gathered together for consultation. Finally, James arose and gave the judgment. This decision was of the Holy Spirit. Because when they wrote the circular letter they could say, "For it seemed good to the Holy Spirit, and to us" (v.28). The judgment came from the Holy Spirit; it had touched spiritual reality. Though the word proceeded from the mouth of James, even so "the apostles and the elders, with the whole church," said amen and agreed to the decision (v.22). This is body life. Body life is lived out when the reality is touched in the Holy Spirit. It is not by fulfilling a certain procedure but by touching reality that body life is truly practiced.

We ought to realize that all spiritual life and teaching has its reality before God. If one has not touched that reality—and no matter how well he may preach the doctrine—he produces nothing of spiritual value. If a person has not touched the reality of the church yet all the while talks about the church, he is in darkness, deceiving himself, and is full of pride. But for that person who has made contact with the spiritual reality, his life is practical and living instead of being in letter and external.

A wonderful thing happens after you touch reality. Whenever you encounter someone who has not touched, or entered into, reality, you immediately sense it. You know he has not touched that reality because he is still following the mind, the law, the rule or regulation. Before God there is something which the Bible calls "true." It is nothing other than "reality." In relating to this trueness—this reality—one is delivered from doctrine, letter, human thoughts, and human ways. Be it baptism or breaking of bread or the church, there is a reality. Nothing is mere form, procedure, or doctrine.

As to the instance of worship, we read these words: "God is a Spirit: and they that worship him must worship in spirit and truth" (John 4.24). The word "truth" means "reality." The emphasis here is on the Spirit, for by the Spirit the reality is brought in. God must be worshiped in spirit. What is of the spirit is real; what is not of the spirit is not real. Worship is not attained by sentiment or feeling or thought. Worship must be in spirit and in truth. What is trueness? When the spirit contacts God, there is trueness; when it does not contact God, there is no trueness, for that which is of the spirit is true while that which is not of the spirit is not true. Besides the kind of worship which is in letter, even that which is called spiritual worship sometimes fails to draw out the response of amen. You may not be able to explain why, but somehow you sense that this is not it. Contrarily, you may be able to say amen to some who worship God in silence, for there you meet the trueness, the reality.

To give thanks and praise is good, yet many thanks and praises are but forms; they are not what the Bible calls trueness or reality. Brothers and sisters, do you not have this experience, that when someone is thanking and praising, deep down within you there is not only no amen but there is icy coldness? The more he gives thanks and praises, the colder you feel inside. Or suppose someone has met up with a difficulty and he is praising and thanking God loudly and profusely as if there were no difficulty. Is this not good? Surely, it is good. But somehow the more he praises, the less you are able to say amen. In your heart you muse that it is right to thank and praise God, yet somehow this praise and thanksgiving do not seem to be the right thing, it is not reality. On the other hand, you may meet another brother who, though he is thanking and praising God, does not do so quite so loudly. He does not appear to be quite as exuberant, his face may look a little sad; and he is thanking and praising the Lord softly. Strange to say, you spontaneously utter an amen. You sense this is the right thing, that he has contacted reality.

INSTANCE 6

As to the example of prayer, we will not consider formal prayers here at all. Nevertheless, some long and seemingly zealous prayers likewise do not draw out an amen. The more such prayers are offered, the colder are our responses. This is due to no other reason than that such prayers have not touched spiritual reality. The eighteenth chapter of Luke's Gospel tells of two men who went to the temple to pray. The publican smote his breast, pleading, "God, be thou merciful to me a sinner." *His* prayer reaches our hearts. But the self-commending Pharisee, who opened his mouth to thank God, does not strike any responsive chord in us. Why? Because the one prayed to God, while the other "prayed thus with himself" (v.11). Many soliloquized prayers not only do not draw out our amen but even nauseate us. Yet true prayers, however short and ineloquent they may be, touch reality; and they in turn touch the deep recesses of men, causing them to naturally respond with an amen.

INSTANCE 7

As to how the blood of the Lord Jesus cleanses our conscience, this problem can never be resolved in the physical realm. Can we ever imagine a person at the time of the crucifixion sprinkling the blood of the Lord Jesus upon his body, thus getting his conscience cleansed? He would not be cleansed by that means at all, for the Holy Spirit is the executor of all spiritual things. When the Holy Spirit cleanses our conscience with the blood He is using the spiritual reality of that blood, not its physical properties, to cleanse us. Only that which is in the Holy Spirit is real. When a person contacts the reality in the Holy Spirit, he touches life. If what he contacts is only doctrine, he will not receive life.

INSTANCE 8

That our old man was crucified with Christ, as declared in Romans 6, is a fact. Some Christians are still saying: "I know my old man was crucified, but I do not understand why this old man of mine is still living day by day." The reason for this is that he has touched only the doctrine; he has yet to encounter the spiritual reality. We ought to realize that if doctrine is in letter but not in the Holy Spirit, it does not give life, no matter how familiar we are with it. Matters such as salvation, justification, and sanctification are dead to us if all we have touched are mere doctrines and letters. That which is in the Holy Spirit is spiritually real. When one touches spiritual reality he obtains life, for it is living and fresh.

Someone may preach a seemingly spiritual message, yet have it cause heaviness to the hearers. This is because what he says is not reality. Had he touched reality, his words would ring true. Solely what is real causes people to touch reality. Otherwise, no matter how well a person speaks, those who know reality will discover its unrealness.

INSTANCE 9

As to the matter of knowing Christ, whatever is known by outward appearance is not true knowledge; only what is known in reality is a true apprehending. While the Lord Jesus was on earth, many men encountered Him. They seemed to have contacted Him; yet they did not.. They seemed to have recognized Him; yet they did not. Such knowledge is external. Those who truly know Christ have all touched reality. Their knowledge is in the spirit. Let us see a bit more of this from the Bible, because it is too basic an experience to be overlooked.

When the Lord Jesus was on earth, He was known in two different ways: He was known by appearance and He was known inwardly.

What is knowing Christ by appearance? This was the kind of knowledge by which the Jews understood Christ. From the very beginning, they assumed a knowing attitude. They announced, "Is not this Jesus, the son of Joseph, whose father and mother we know?" (John 6.42) They were pretty sure they knew Him. They knew even His father and mother. Once when the Lord Jesus came to His own country, the people remarked: "Is not this the carpenter, the son of Mary, and brother of James, and Joses, and Judas, and Simon? and are not his sisters here with us?" (Mark 6.3) They knew not only His father and mother but also His brothers and sisters. Yet did they actually know the Lord Jesus? No, they did not. Though they knew His father and mother, they did not recognize the Lord Himself. Although they knew His brothers and sisters, they did not know Him. They judged the Lord Jesus by appearance; they did not touch the reality.

There was another class of people whose knowledge of the Lord was somewhat deeper than that of the Jews, but still they did not perceive Him in an inward way. Once when the Lord Jesus came into the parts of Caesarea Philippi, He asked His disciples, saying, "Who do men say that the Son of man is?" And they said, "Some say John the Baptist; some, Elijah; and others, Jeremiah, or one of the prophets" (Matt. 16.13-14). Their knowledge of the Lord was certainly more advanced than that of the Jews.

Some said the Lord was Elijah. Elijah was a powerful prophet; it might be said that Elijah stood for power. The Lord Jesus was certainly an Elijah, the most powerful of the prophets. Some said the Lord was Jeremiah. Jeremiah was a weeping prophet; he was representative of passion. The Lord Jesus was indeed a Jeremiah also, for He too was full of passion. Seven times He denounced the hypocritical Pharisees and Scribes with woes (Matt. 23.13,15,16,23,15,17,19). When He found those in the temple who sold oxen and sheep and doves, and when He saw the changers of money sitting, He cast all of them out of the temple, including the sheep and oxen; and He in addition poured out the changers' money and overthrew their tables (John 2.14-15). He was truly an Elijah. But when Jesus was with the publicans and sinners, He sat at table with them (Matt. 9.10). While He was sitting at the table in the house of Simon, He allowed a sinful woman to cry at His feet (Luke 7.37-38). In seeing Mary weeping and the Jews also weeping, He groaned in His spirit and wept (John 11.33,35). He was truly a Jeremiah. Nonetheless, when people confessed that He was Elijah or Jeremiah, they revealed that they knew Him no more than by appearance.

At first the early disciples also only knew the Lord in the flesh. They did not have that inward recognition of Him yet. People like Thomas and Philip were with the Lord for quite some time. Humanly speaking, they ought to have really known the Lord, but alas, they did not. When the Lord spoke openly, "And whither I go, ye know the way," Thomas said to Him, "Lord, we know not whither thou goest; how know we the way?" (John 14.4-5). To the clear statement of the Lord, "If ye had known me, ye would have known my Father also: from henceforth ye know him, and have seen him," Philip answered, "Lord, show us the Father, and it sufficeth us" (John 14.7-8). The Lord Jesus whom Thomas perceived was but a man of Nazareth; he did not yet comprehend the Lord Jesus as the Lord of life. What Philip saw in the Lord Jesus was likewise but a Nazarene; he did not see the Lord Jesus as the other form of the Father. Though both had been with the Lord Jesus, their knowledge of Him remained external because they had not touched the reality.

The disciples knew the Lord Jesus more than the Jews; even so, they had to learn what a Lord He was. After having been with Him for such a long period, they failed to recognize Him as He really was. They saw Him with their own eyes, heard Him with their own ears, touched Him with their own hands, yet they knew Him not. This indicates to us that to know the Lord requires an organ sharper than the optic sense, keener than the auditory sense, and more sensitive than the tactile sense. In Christ there is a reality which cannot be recognized in the flesh.

Peter's knowledge of the Lord on that particular day in Caesarea Philippi was an inward knowing. When the Lord asked His disciples, "But who say ye that I am?", Simon Peter answered with, "Thou are the Christ, the Son of the living God." Immediately the Lord declared, "Blessed art thou, Simon Bar-Jonah: for flesh and blood hath not revealed it unto thee, but my Father who is in heaven" (Matt. 16.15-17). What the Lord meant was: though you have followed Me for some time, your former knowledge was deficient; your knowledge today, however, is most blessed, for this has come rather through the revelation of My heavenly Father. This knowledge is real.

For this reason, unless there be revelation, men do not recognize who the Lord is, even if they may have eaten and drunk with Him or walked and stayed with Him. Without this revealed knowledge, all which is known of Him is but the external Christ, the historical Christ. This is termed a knowing of Christ after the flesh. Only the knowledge of Christ as Peter experienced through revelation is real and can be said to be apprehending Christ inwardly.

"Wherefore we henceforth know no man after the flesh: even though we have known Christ after the flesh, yet now we know him so no more" (2 Cor. 5.16). During the days of his knowing Christ after the flesh, Paul dared to attack the name of Jesus of Nazareth and to persecute and ill-treat the disciples of the Lord (Acts 26.9-11). But after God revealed His Son in Paul's spirit, he preached the faith of which he had once made havoc (Gal. 1.16,23). He became a different person. This new knowledge he now had was spiritual reality; he therefore no longer knew Christ after the flesh.

The Gospel according to Mark includes the record of a woman who had had an issue of blood twelve years. "Having heard the things concerning Jesus, (she) came in the crowd behind, and touched his garment . . . And straightway the fountain of her blood was dried up; and she felt in her body that she was healed of her plague." What did the Lord feel at that moment? "Who touched my garments?" He asked. But the disciples answered, "Thou seest the multitude thronging thee, and sayest thou, Who touched me?" (Mark 5.27-31) Here we see two classes of people: those who touch Him and those who throng Him. The latter can only throng against the Christ in the flesh; the former, however, can touch the Christ in His reality. The Lord does not seem to be aware of those who throng Him, but He is very conscious of the touch of those who really touch Him. How sad that there are multitudes who throng Him, yet only one who touches Him!

> *But of a truth I say unto you, There were many widows in Israel in the days of Elijah, when the heaven was shut up three years and six months, when there came a great famine over all the land; and unto none of them was Elijah sent, but only to Zarephath, in the land of Sidon, unto a woman that was a widow. And there were many lepers in Israel in the time of Elisha the prophet; and none of them was cleansed, but only Naaman the Syrian. (Luke 4.25-27)*

These episodes are similar to the story of the woman cleansed of her issue of blood. The question lies not in distance (how far or how near), nor in time (how permanent or how transient), but in who is thronging and who is touching reality.

Unless a person has touched reality, he will remain unchanged no matter how closely he may throng against the Lord.

He who knows Christ after the flesh will never actually recognize Him. Only by revelation can a person discern Christ. We need to remember that Christ is not known by our outward senses—such as optical, auditory, and tactile. Knowing Christ is the work of the Holy Spirit. Without the Holy Spirit, no one can apprehend the reality of Christ. However familiar one may be with the history of the Lord Jesus, and no matter if one may have thronged the Lord, heard His voice, and knelt before Him, he has not touched the reality of Christ before God if he does not have the Holy Spirit.

"The words that I have spoken unto you are spirit, and are life" (John 6.63). A person who has touched the Holy Spirit has life. It is utterly impossible for one to touch the Spirit without possessing life. What is of the Spirit is life. Touching reality is possessing life. It is just here that many problems arise. Some come to know the Lord by reading books, others by hearing people. Whether it is through reading or through hearing, they have not touched the Lord Himself. The Christ of reality is beyond comparison with the Christ read or heard. This Christ can only be apprehended in the Holy Spirit; there is absolutely no other way of knowing Him.

Many Christians are discouraged because their faith does not seem to work. They complain that they have heard the Word for many years and know a lot, but all of what they know is ineffectual. And why? Because they have not contacted the reality. Touching Christ with the hand of the flesh will never be effective. Power proceeded from Christ to the woman who touched Him. But only one person really touched Him. Whether faith is operative or not depends on whether it has touched reality.

We should understand of course that Christ in the flesh *is* touchable, visible, and audible to the hands, eyes, and ears of the flesh. But Christ in the Holy Spirit can only be reached in the Holy Spirit. Even while the Lord Jesus lived on earth, there were the external and inward knowings of Him already. Our knowledge of Him today is no different from that of the past. The question is, therefore, How do we know Christ? If one day we see Him by the Holy Spirit and hence touch the Christ of spiritual reality, then on that day we know Him inwardly even though we may not be able to speak or to explain. Once we see inwardly, all our doubts are resolved. For this reason, we must ask the Lord to give us a true knowledge of Him—a seeing which does not come from ourselves nor from the instruction of flesh and blood but from the revelation of the heavenly Father.

INSTANCE 10

It is right for a brother to forgive another brother. Now sometimes you see a brother forgiving another brother who has offended him: how he tries his best to forgive, how loudly he announces his forgiveness. Judging by outward appearance, he really forgives most generously; yet somehow you do not feel right inside. You feel he is trying too hard to forgive. His is not the real thing. Why? Because he has not touched the reality. You may, however, meet another brother. He has also been hurt by a brother. He is saddened, yet he believes that God cannot be wrong: he therefore feels he must forgive his brother from his heart. But he does not proclaim his forgiveness with a loud voice nor express how transcendent he is. He simply says that he forgives his brother. You sense this brother is not acting but is truly forgiving. This brother has touched spiritual reality.

INSTANCE 11

Humility ought to impress people. But the humility of some Christians makes you feel they are using their own strength to be humble. One may exclaim endlessly how undone he is, yet you sense that his is a "voluntary humility"— that is, will-humility or humility of the will. (Col. 2.18,23). The humility he projects is not the genuine article. If he is proud, you may call it pride, for this humility of his you do not know exactly how to label. You cannot say it is pride nor can you say it is humility. His outward attitude resembles humility, yet it is far from the real thing.

But there may be another brother who does not use his own strength and will to be humble. He instead acts naturally and speaks softly, and the result is that immediately *your* pride is uncovered. You sense how shameful your pride is. If in any given situation the other party is proud, you too can be proud. But if he esteems others as more excellent than himself, then he will seek the help of others so naturally. He has touched the reality of humility.

INSTANCE 12

As to the instance of love, the thirteenth chapter of 1 Corinthians furnishes us with a most distinct picture. "And if I bestow all my goods to feed the poor, and if I give my body to be burned" (v.3). From the human point of view, rarely is there a man with such love. It may be said that there is no love greater than this. Yet Paul says, "but have not love, it profiteth me nothing" (v.3). It means that there is the possibility of not having love in spite of the fact of bestowing all one's goods to the poor and giving one's body to be burned. In other words, except a person touches the reality of love in the Holy Spirit, his is but an outward conduct. It is possible for a brother to give away all his goods to feed the poor and to give up his body to be burned without having love in him. It is also possible for a brother to "give to drink unto one of these little ones a cup of cold water only" and to receive his reward (Matt. 10.42). The issue here is not how much or how little is done but whether or not the reality is touched. Only that reality which is contacted by the Spirit of the Lord is real.

May we see that we need not act more than what we are before God. Some express such great love that it causes people to doubt if it is genuine. Some Christians show such love but it is void of human feeling; this arouses suspicion. As we read 2 Corinthians we see how Paul was misunderstood and slandered, how he suffered and was embarrassed; but he overcame all these things. He was not without feeling, however, for he was a real man. He was distressed, but he overcame. He suffered, but he overcame. Nonetheless, his victory is the victory of man, not the victory of an angel. He really overcame, but he overcame as a human being. He was truly human, and his victory was also real. By the Spirit of God he touched the reality. When we read his words we cannot but bow our heads and say, "Here is a man who is not far from us. We seem to be able to touch him." We feel he is not like Michael or Gabriel, that he does not live among the cherubim but is a knowable person. This is due to no other reason than that he has spiritual reality. Consequently, in touching him we touch life.

chapter 2

spiritual reality: its relationships

(1) Reality and Conduct

We ought to remember that there is a thing before God called reality. The difficulty with many Christians is that they try to manufacture it. They attempt to produce this reality before God. With the result that they copy or imitate. What God requires, though, is trueness—the real thing manifested in our lives. That which we do by ourselves is manmade, a counterfeit, and not the genuine thing. How very vain it is for man to act on the basis of doctrine, for all he has is nothing more than an outward conduct. He does not have the true article—the reality.

Because of this, we must learn to live before God according to what we verily are. We should ask Him to cause us to contact that which is spiritually real. Sometimes we are close to being false simply because we know too much and ac·

according to doctrines, instead of following the leading of God's Spirit. Whenever we act on the basis of doctrine we are not touching reality.

Once a brother narrated his experience as follows: a brother of mine had greatly offended me. One day he came to talk with me and I said, "Brother, it does not matter, there is nothing to it." But deep down in me was a feeling which said, "This matter is not right, for he always does such things. He has done it to many others as well as to me." I felt I should seriously reprimand him. But I reasoned that if I should gravely reprove him he might be hurt and say that I would not forgive him. If instead I were to shake hands with him and invite him to a meal, would this not show that I could love the brother? Nevertheless, there was a strong conviction within me, saying, "You must speak the truth to him today. Show him wherein his conduct is wrong." After having struggled within for over fifteen minutes, I finally spoke the truth to him.

It is a fact that sometimes it is more valuable to reprove than to shake hands. Though we may maintain a gentle appearance which causes people to praise us, there is no spiritual value before God. The question is: does our conduct follow the dictate of dead doctrine or of the leading of the Holy Spirit? The above-mentioned brother genuinely loved his brother in his heart, yet the issue was not over the heart but over spiritual reality.

One day a Christian had a strife with one of the members of his family. The latter, being very violent, struck the Christian's face. At that moment the brother remembered what Matthew 5 instructs: "Whosoever smiteth thee on thy right cheek, turn to him the other also" (v.39). He thought that being a Christian he ought to act like one, so he turned the other cheek. Having done it, he was so exasperated afterwards that he could not sleep for two nights. As far as his conduct went he had acted in accordance with the word of the Bible. Nevertheless he was so enraged that for two nights he lost his sleep. This plainly betrays the fact that he had not touched the spiritual reality. His conduct was not out of life; it was not the real thing.

Many Christians sense that they have a deficiency in that they are unable to distinguish true from false, unable to discern what is of God and what is not of God. The reason for such a deficiency, judging from spiritual experience, lies in their failure to have touched spiritual reality. Had they made contact with that reality, then the moment any unreal thing might appear before their eyes they would instantly recognize it for what it was. The power of discerning comes out of what one has already seen. If we have touched spiritual reality in a certain matter, no one can ever deceive us in that particular matter. A truly saved believer has at least touched the spiritual reality of salvation. It is consequently difficult to deceive him in this matter. Similarly, he who has touched the spiritual reality of a certain matter will only naturally detect the unreal thing as soon as it appears. And as he encounters the counterfeit, there arises a strange power within him which pushes away the counterfeit.

The reason we are so easily deceived is because we often deceive ourselves. The self-deceived are prone to be deceived by others. If we do not see something in ourselves, how can we see it in others? It is when we come to know ourselves that we commence to know others. None who do not know themselves are able to know others. But once having come through God's dealing to see what we are, we naturally recognize what others are. If in a particular matter you have received God's dealing and touched the reality, you know how the Spirit of God

works in you. By this knowledge you instantly discern
whether another person is acting on his own or is moved by
the Spirit of God.

Spiritual discernment comes only after we ourselves have
contacted the reality. The one who has not touched reality
deceives two persons: himself, and the one who is spiritually in
the same category. He cannot deceive those who know what is
of the Holy Spirit and who live in the Holy Spirit. He has
absolutely no way to deceive the church. He may consider
himself spiritual, but for some unknown reason the church
does not say amen. We know that whenever the church does
not amen a person, it is time for that person to confess his sin.
If brothers and sisters do not feel like saying amen, that person
must have falsehood in him.

Some brothers and sisters trouble and burden the church
not simply with their sins but also with their "good"—that
which issues from themselves. Sin is easily recognized, but the
"good" which proceeds from self is not so easily detected,
though it is far from God and far from spiritual reality. It is a
matter of great concern to behold how often Christians regard
themselves as having come into some certain thing after they
have labored over it, when in actuality they have not yet
touched its spiritual reality. We believe that when one encounters reality, it will result in life; but when one does not
encounter reality, it will end in death. One brother performs a
particular act before God; he touches life and causes others to
touch life. Another brother also takes a certain action; he feels
he has done well; yet others do not meet life in him—and they
are not edified. Instead of admiring his action, they reject it. It
is because this brother's conduct comes out of himself; and the
consequence is death instead of life.

We must learn to live in the Holy Spirit, otherwise we may

exercise "good" conduct without touching the spiritual reality. What is meant by living in the Holy Spirit? It means not doing anything by or out from ourselves. Whatever is done by the self is of the flesh, and whatever is of the flesh is definitely not spiritual reality. Spiritual reality is spiritual, not fleshly. To put it simply, spiritual reality is what one touches by the Holy Spirit. The thing which that one so touches is living and real. The conduct of a Christian is not real if it is not in the Holy Spirit. His conduct can never be a substitute for the real thing before God. It can neither help others nor edify himself. May God be merciful to us that we may realize that to live in the Holy Spirit is to live in spiritual reality.

(2) Supply and Reality

2 Corinthians 4 especially shows us how there is supply where there is reality. "Always bearing about in the body the dying of Jesus, that the life also of Jesus may be manifested in our body" (v.10). Where the dying of Jesus is exhibited, there is the manifestation of the life of Jesus. In other words, since the dying of Jesus is in us, the life of Jesus is also in us. This refers to those who know the dying of Jesus and in whom the life of Jesus is manifested.

"So then death worketh in us, but life in you" (v.12). In verse 10, Paul speaks of the manifestation of life; here in verse 12, he speaks of the supply of life. That which is manifested in us we call life, but that which is manifested in others we call supply. The source is the same, since all come from the dying of Jesus. Consequently, preaching without reality is empty and useless, because it cannot supply the body of Christ. Only after the dying of Jesus has worked in us can the life of Jesus work in others. Hence this is more than a matter of preaching or working, but is a matter of the supply of life.

Of course preaching has its proper place, but if it is not backed up by reality it cannot supply life. When we bear in our bodies the dying of Jesus the body of Christ receives the supply. Where there is reality, there is supply. If we do not know "the dying of Jesus" and have not quietly borne the cross, then we will have no supply. Brothers and sisters, please remember that so far as spiritual reality is concerned, work is not what you *do* but what you have *passed through* before God; it is this which will automatically supply the body of Christ. If you know on your side what the dying of Jesus is, the church on the other side will spontaneously receive supply.

Because of this, we do not need to tell people that we have forgiven this or that, nor blow the trumpet that we have loved, nor draw people's attention to how we have borne the cross. If we have touched reality we will effortlessly supply other people. It does not matter if we are conscious of it or not. The fact remains: "death worketh in us, but life in you."

Our difficulty lies in our knowing too much of teachings. We act according to teaching, but there is no practical supply. Let us remember that supply is not an outward act but an inward reality. If you had known before God what the dying of Jesus is, then the life of Jesus would spontaneously work in the church. Where life is, there is supply, for supply is the imparting of life, not the exhibiting of work to be admired. Supply is to build up people, not to build up the reputation that you have had such and such an experience. What is important is whether or not there is real supply. Each time you pass through "the dying of Jesus" some brothers or sisters will receive from you the supply of life. There is no need to wait until you publish your autobiography.

At the time we receive life from the Lord, at that time the church is already being supplied with life. We need to know that many helps given transcend consciousness and feeling. When we have reality people will be supplied whether we are conscious of it or not, for life is a fact. Whenever we are truly bearing the cross before the Lord, the body of Christ receives the supply.

How can we comprehend what Paul says—"So then death worketh in us but life in you"—if we are ignorant of what the supply of life is? Paul tells the saints in Colossae, "Now I rejoice in my sufferings for your sake, and fill up on my part that which is lacking of the afflictions of Christ in my flesh for his body's sake, which is the church" (1.24). What is this? It is the supply of life. Having seen the body of Christ as one, there will naturally be supply. Hence Paul is able to suffer for the sake of the body of Christ and to fill up on his part in his flesh that which is lacking of the afflictions of Christ. You cannot understand how the afflictions of Christ can be filled up if you have not seen that the body of Christ is one.

Let us ask the Lord to open our eyes to see that the body is one. Whosoever really knows that the body is one cannot fail to see 1 Corinthians 4.7: "What hast thou that thou didst not receive?" All we have has been received from God, and all is for the supply of the body. The reality we personally touch before God becomes the supply of the church.

The supply of the body exceeds the physical restrictions of communication. Paul says to the church in Corinth: "For I verily, being absent in body but present in spirit" (1 Cor. 5.3). Because he has touched the reality of the body of Christ, therefore he may say his spirit is present with them just as his body was present with them before. This is no idealism; it is reality. Our having seen the oneness of the body of Christ, our spirit invariably is found there. This is called the supply of life, and it transcends words and works and surpasses the limitations of physical communication. If we know God and are in contact with the Lord, whatever we pass through automatically becomes the wealth of the body.

What a pity that many Christians live in the external realm! When they work, there seems to be some supply; but when they are not working, there is no supply. When they open their mouths, they appear to be God's choice servants; but when their mouths are shut, they are no longer God's choice servants. They are able to supply when they are appreciated, but cannot supply when they are misunderstood. Because they have not touched spiritual reality before God, they fail to supply life to the body of Christ. Yet there are those who are such that when people talk with them for but five minutes, those people receive a life supply through them. The body of Christ is a fact. Spiritual supply does not depend on shaking hands nor on conversation. If anyone has gone through some experience before God—having received from God's hand "the dying of Jesus"—he has already supplied the body of Christ.

Brothers and sisters, we supply the church with what we have known of God within. It is not that we try to supply, nor purposely aim at supplying the body of Christ, but that we are just naturally supplying the church. He who has touched reality has supply; he who has not touched reality does not have supply. It is something which cannot be forced. Judging from the experience of Paul, we can truly say that supplying the body of Christ is a reality and not an act. If we have experienced reality before God, we will spontaneously supply the church with that reality. Only when we have real experience do we benefit the church.

The words which Paul says are quite unique. We easily

understand when he says, "always bearing about in the body
the dying of Jesus, that the life also of Jesus may be manifested in our body." But when he says this—"so then death
worketh in us, but life in you"—we do not so easily comprehend its meaning, not unless we know the oneness of the body
of Christ. Since the body is one, whatever works in me will
naturally work in others. This is life and this is supply. Upon
seeing this, we are exceedingly joyful because all which the
members receive from the Head is kept in the body. And we
all are enjoying this body.

Brothers and sisters, if we have touched this reality, we will
not bemoan the poverty and barrenness of the church. Doubtless, so far as appearance goes, we have to acknowledge the
poor and degraded condition of the church. We must confess
that in outward appearance individual Christian groups as well
as individual Christians have all failed. But whenever we touch
the *reality* of the church, we immediately declare that the
church is neither poor nor degraded. It is not because of the
failure of individual Christians and individual Christian groups
that the wealth of the church is diminished, for day by day all
which the members receive from the Head is supplying the
church. Paul touched this spiritual reality; thus he could reprove the church in Corinth as well as supply their needs.

"Till we all attain unto the unity of the faith, and of the
knowledge of the Son of God, unto a full-grown man, unto the
measure of the stature of the fulness of Christ" (Eph. 4.13).
This word is rather difficult to understand outwardly and
mentally. For the church to attain to the unity of the faith
seems something far distant and beyond the realm of possibility when we look at outward appearance. Who knows if the
church will ever arrive at that point? Yet when we touch
spiritual reality, we do not sense the need to ask such a

question. We know that the church before God is one and has never been divided. As soon as we touch the reality, all external questions disappear. How can we supply if we have not seen this reality? Our supply begins the moment we see it. Hence supply is based on touching the reality of the body as well as on the experience of the cross.

Let us realize too that the supply of words is also based on the life we have already given to the church. Brothers and sisters, the Holy Spirit will bear witness to what you express if what you say is what you already have given the church in life. But He will not bear witness to what you utter if it does not represent what you have received before God. People receive help from your words only if you have first supplied them with your life. Otherwise the help which words give is merely a bit of clarification for the mind, since such help is but the produce of the tree of the knowledge of good and evil. The food of the church, though, is life. The supply of life is the one and only food of the church. The question is not what you can give, but how much you already have given to the church. What have you given of reality to the church? When you stand before the church, what is it that you have already supplied to her? If you have not touched reality, you will have nothing to supply the people. Only what is spiritual, which has reality behind the word, can supply the church.

Some Christians deem "the body of Christ" to be only a parable. They have not seen the reality of the body, and therefore have no way to supply it. There is no possibility of supplying the body if one has not seen it. It is with the body in view that the eating of the mouth is the eating of the body, the seeing of the eyes is the seeing of the body, and the hearing of the ears is the hearing of the body. What a member receives, the body receives. No matter which brother or sister it is, whatever he or she receives is also received by the body. We need to understand that body life is not only a corporate living but a corporate life as well. If we fail to touch this reality, the church is but a doctrine and the body a parable; accordingly, we have no way to supply the need.

Brothers and sisters, do not forget that you are not an independent entity but a member in the body. "And whether one member suffereth," says Paul, "all the members suffer with it, or one member is honored, all the members rejoice with it" (1 Cor. 12.26). Is this empty word or fact? Paul is a man who has body-consciousness. If he had not touched the reality of the body, he would not be able to utter such a word. Let us therefore ask God to cause us to touch the root, which is the reality, that we may spontaneously supply the church.

(3) Question and Reality

If we have not seen spiritual reality we will obviously have many questions. Suppose, for example, you hear things said about a person whom you have never met. Naturally you will make inquiry about him from those who know him. But there is one person in this whole world whom you already know thoroughly without need of any inquiry. That person is your own self. You yourself are a reality which you know. Or again, suppose there is available for occupancy a house which you have never seen before. To know about it you have to ask how many rooms it has, whether the windows are large enough, etc., etc. But once you move into it and live there, you have no further questions to ask. Whatever is already clear need not be asked any more. In other words, if we live in the reality of a thing we have no more questions. Only a person who does not know the body of Christ will ask what it is. He who knows will not ask such a question.

With regard to spiritual matters, we can clarify them to the extent of removing any spiritual difficulty, but we cannot make them so clear as to present no problem to the human mind. Take preaching the gospel as an example: we can preach till people are clear enough to believe, but we cannot preach till man's mind is fully satisfied. What did Nathanael say when Philip told him that they had found Him of whom Moses in the law and the prophets had written? Said he, "Can any good thing come out of Nazareth?" Yet later, when the Lord said to him, "Before Philip called thee, when thou wast under the fig tree, I saw thee," Nathanael encountered reality. Whereupon he most naturally confessed, "Thou art the Son of God; thou art King of Israel" (John 1.45-49). He had touched reality, and hence he had no more question. This is how spiritual things are. As soon as one touches reality, he is enlightened within. He knows inwardly, whether or not he is able to explain it.

Some passages in the Bible appear to be easily misunderstood. But if the Holy Spirit is present, one is able to contact the spiritual reality. With this, there can be no misunderstanding.

chapter 3

spiritual reality:
how to enter in

Oftentimes spiritual reality is nothing more than terminology to us for we have not yet entered into the reality of it. Only after we have entered in can we touch that which is real. Hence the question becomes, How can we enter into spiritual reality? "Howbeit when he, the Spirit of truth, is come, he shall guide you into all the truth . . . He shall glorify me: for he shall take of mine, and shall declare it unto you" (John 16.13-14). These two verses tell us that it is the Holy Spirit who declares truth to us and guides us into all of it.

Of all the works of the Holy Spirit, two are of prime importance; namely, the revelation of the Spirit, and the discipline of the Spirit. The first enables us to know and to see spiritual reality, while the second guides us into the experience of spiritual reality through environmental arrangements.

Revelation is the foundation of all spiritual progress. Without the revelation of the Holy Spirit, no matter how good one's knowledge and how excellent one's outward conduct, that Christian remains superficial before God and may never have advanced even one step forward. On the other hand, if one has a revelation of the Holy Spirit and yet lacks the additional discipline of the Holy Spirit, that Christian's life is incomplete. We may say that the revelation of the Holy Spirit is the foundation while the discipline of the Holy Spirit is the construction. This does not mean that there is a period called the revelation of the Holy Spirit and then another period called the discipline of the Holy Spirit. The two are mingled. When He reveals, He also disciplines; and while He disciplines, He likewise reveals. For this reason, revelation does not embrace the whole of the Christian life unless it also includes discipline.

We believe whatsoever the Father has entrusted to the Son, the Son has accomplished (John 17.4). We also believe that whatsoever the Son has entrusted to the Holy Spirit, the Holy Spirit will accomplish. We believe that however immense spiritual reality is, the Holy Spirit is well able to guide us into such an immense reality. There is nothing whatsoever of Christ which has been kept from the church. This involves not only our experience, but even more so it involves the question of whether the work of the Holy Spirit is successful. Let us bear in mind that as Christ has accomplished all, so too shall the Holy Spirit accomplish all. We must believe the trustworthiness of the Spirit and the completeness of His work.

The object of the Holy Spirit's work is to guide us into trueness, into reality. He gives us revelation in order to bring us into the presence of trueness that we may see what we are in Christ. Some Christians have a defect, as if the Holy Spirit has very little organization—very little incorporation— in them. When they do not have enough to help themselves, how can they be expected to help other people? They can barely supply their own need; it is out of the question for them to supply others. A Christian who wishes to help others must himself be brought by the Spirit of the Lord into reality. In order to guide him into spiritual reality, the Spirit of the Lord must lead him into much discipline and many trials.

"O God of my righteousness: in pressure thou hast enlarged me" (Ps. 4.1 Darby). God allowed David to fall into distress that He might lead him into enlargement. In his epistle the apostle James says this: "Hearken, my beloved brethren, did not God choose them that are poor as to the world to be rich in faith, and heirs of the kingdom which he promised to them that love him?" (2.5) God chooses the poor in the world that they may be rich in faith. God does not entertain the idea of having His children always in distress and in poverty. His aim is to lead them from distress into enlargement, from poverty to richness in faith.

Revelation 21 shows us what the condition of the church shall be before God when she appears in the future. "Having the glory of God: her (the holy city, Jerusalem) light was like unto a stone most precious, as it were a jasper stone, clear as crystal" (v.11). "And the building of the wall thereof was jasper: and the city was pure gold, like unto pure glass. The foundations of the wall of the city were adorned with all manner of precious stones" (vv.18-19). "And the city lieth foursquare, and the length thereof is as great as the breadth: and he measured the city with the reed, twelve thousand furlongs: the length and the breadth and the height thereof are equal" (v.16). How rich and how enlarged the church is when she shall one day appear before God.

What is enlargement? The enlargement which the psalmist speaks of is when in distress you are brought by God into an enlarged place to enjoy Him. Distress is not able to depress you. He who enjoys the company of the Fourth Person in the fiery furnace (Daniel 3.25) is he who enjoys God; and he who enjoys God is an enlarged person. The one who is cast into prison with his feet fast in the stocks and yet can pray and sing hymns to God (Acts 16.24-25) is he who enjoys God; such a one is certainly being enlarged. A person shut behind prison bars but still enjoying the presence of the Lord must inevitably be an enlarged person.

The Holy Spirit aims at leading us to enlargement through distress; but, sad to say, sometimes we instead are overwhelmed by distress. We have seen the end or purpose of the Lord in the case of Job, of how the Lord is full of pity and merciful (James 5.11). Job indeed realized the end of the Lord, but some come to an end before the end of the Lord is reached! They are pressed by distress and fail to come into an enlarged place. As soon as they are tested, they murmur and accuse God of being unfair; consequently they are capsized by distress, never taking the opportunity of being brought into enlargement.

Some Christians though not in distress may be in poverty. They lack spiritual reality. What they have is insufficient to supply their own need; how can they ever talk about helping other people? But, thank God, there are Christians who are spiritually rich. Of such ones you cannot fathom their depth nor measure their breadth. Whenever you have trouble, you go to them and you are always helped. It seems as if you could never encounter a problem about which they did not know something and that a person could never go to them without being helped. You have to bow your head and say, "Thank God, there are such rich people in the church." Their wealth exceeds your poverty, hence they can supply your need. They are rich because they have touched reality.

Whether a church is able to be a golden candlestick, that is, whether it can really testify for the Lord, depends on how many enlarged Christians there are in the church, on how many Christians are rich in faith, and on how much Christians can supply other people. It is true, we can go and knock on the door of a friend at midnight and borrow three loaves when we have nothing to set before another friend who has come to us from a journey (Luke 11.5-6). Yet, sometimes when people need bread, the Lord will tell us, "Give *ye* them to eat" (Matt. 14.16). How many loaves do we really have? Oftentimes we may pray in an emergency and God is merciful to us. Nevertheless, emergency prayer cannot substitute for richness. How poor we are if there is no increase in spiritual things after, say, a year or five years!

What is the cause of poverty? The lack of the discipline and control of the Holy Spirit is its cause. Let us recognize that all those who are enlarged and rich before God are people who have gone through things and who have a history with God. Their experiences and their history make the church rich. Many sicknesses are for the wealth of the church; many difficulties are for the wealth of the church; many sufferings are for the wealth of the church; and many frustrations are for the wealth of the church.

Look at the number of Christians who pass their days peacefully and at ease. The outcome is spiritual poverty. When other brothers and sisters are in trouble, they do not understand nor are they able to offer any spiritual assistance. They have no history before God. The Holy Spirit has no opportunity to manifest the reality of Christ in them because He has no chance to incorporate Christ in them. However much they may have heard the Word, hearing cannot substitute for the work of the Holy Spirit. To those who lack the work of the

Spirit in their lives, the wealth of Christ does not become their wealth; they therefore have nothing with which to supply other people.

Whether we are useful in God's hand or not is determined by how much the Holy Spirit has worked in us. A Christian ought not be so fallen that the Holy Spirit never seems to have bothered him. His poverty seems predestined, but we believe that the Lord would not let anyone go if that one were to commit himself into the Lord's hand. We believe that each and every trial is for the purpose of enlargement and wealth. Each trial produces more wealth. Every difficulty helps us to know God better. And thus shall we be able to supply the needs of God's children.

One sister was saved when she was thirteen; she lived to be one hundred and three. A brother visited her in her hundredth year and asked why God kept her so long on this earth. She quietly answered: "God keeps me here that I may pray once more, and once more." Oh, how rich she was! Another sister was sick in bed for forty years, and for thirty-five of these years she was deaf. When a brother went to see her, she said: "I was formerly very active, running hither and thither; I did not fulfill the many works of prayer needed by the church. But today I lie in bed. For forty years I daily do the work of prayer." She was not angry nor anxious nor murmuring because of her sickness; instead she did a very good work. Distress had enlarged her and made her rich. And her richness had become the wealth of the church.

Some brothers and sisters are not eloquent in the church nor do they have much knowledge, nonetheless they know how to pray. Whenever they hear anything, they pray for that thing. They pray for the sick, they pray for brothers and sisters in troubles, they supply the church constantly with their prayers. Other brothers and sisters only assemble but never pray, they listen to messages yet do not pray; they have nothing with which to supply the church. They are poor because they have not received the discipline of the Holy Spirit and so do not know what spiritual reality is. Humanly speaking, some brothers and sisters should have fallen away long ago, but they still stand. And the explanation? Because somebody else is supplying them. For this reason, the abundance of life is not a matter of word nor a matter of doctrine but is a matter of how much you have gone through before God and therefore how much you can supply the church.

Day after day the Holy Spirit seeks opportunity to guide us into spiritual reality. If we refuse to accept the discipline of the Holy Spirit, we deny to Him the opportunity to lead us into spiritual reality. All too frequently, when difficulty arises, some people choose the easy way out. When trial arrives, some go around it. Thus is the difficulty avoided, but so also is the opportunity lost for the Holy Spirit to guide into spiritual reality. The Spirit of the Lord has no chance to work something into them so that they may impart to the church what they receive. If we evade the discipline of the Holy Spirit we cannot expect to enter into spiritual reality. And consequently, we miss the opportunity for enlargement and richness.

Brothers and sisters, let us accept the discipline of the Holy Spirit. Then shall we enter into an enlarged place and have something to supply the church. We need once again to consecrate ourselves more completely and more thoroughly so as to give the Spirit of the Lord a chance to perfect His work and to guide us into spiritual reality. May we daily learn before God so that our deposit may become the wealth of the church. Such richness shall one day be manifested in the new heaven and the new earth. Brothers and sisters, there is no gold which has not passed through fire, no precious stone that has not gone through darkness, and no pearl that has not encountered suffering. Let us ask the Lord to deliver us from all vain talk and poverty. Let us ask instead that we may see more and more what spiritual reality is—that we may be guided by His Spirit into all spiritual reality.

chapter 4

obsession: what it is

Who is among you that feareth Jehovah, that obeyeth the voice of his servant? he that walketh in darkness, and hath no light, let him trust in the name of Jehovah, and rely upon his God. Behold, all ye that kindle a fire, that gird yourselves about with firebrands; walk ye in the flame of your fire, and among the brands that ye have kindled. This shall ye have of my hand; ye shall lie down in sorrow. (Is. 50.10-11) For with thee is the fountain of life: In thy light shall we see light. (Ps. 36.9)

Spiritual reality is trueness. It is the truth which sets us free. Oftentimes a Christian fails to touch trueness and falls into falsehood instead. He is deceived and bound by falsehood. He does not clearly see the true character of a thing; yet he considers himself clear. What he thinks and does is wrong, but he reckons himself to be most right. Such a condition we call "obsession." The obsessed person needs the light of God; otherwise he will not be able to come out of his obsession. Let us now see what obsession is.

Obsession is self-deception. 1 John 1.8 describes an obsessed person, declaring him to be self-deceived. If a person knows he has sinned but nevertheless tells others he has not, it is a lie. But if he has sinned and yet believes himself to have no sin, it is self-deception. A lie is committed when one knows in himself that he has sinned but he tells others that he has not. An obsession is evident when one has sinned and yet he thinks so well of himself that he believes himself to be sinless as the Lord Jesus. A liar knows his sin but tries to deceive others. An obsessed person, though he himself has sin, believes and tells others that he has no sin. In other words, what deceives others is a lie while that which deceives oneself is an obsession.

The substance in a lie is the same as in an obsession, both being sin. But in a lie the person knows his sin in his conscience yet intends to deceive others by saying that he has not sinned, whereas in obsession he not only says he has no sin but also psychologically believes in his innocence. He who deceives people is a liar; he who deceives himself is obsessed. All the obsessed deceive themselves. They live in their imagination. Many of those who are proud are obsessed! The proud tend to conceive such thoughts of themselves as to literally believe that they are such as they imagine and to desire others also to believe them to be so.

Paul was once obsessed. When Stephen was stoned to death, Paul "was consenting to his death" (Acts 8.1a). He was completely obsessed within. When he wrote to the church in Philippi, he referred to his former history by saying, "as touching zeal, persecuting the church" (3.6). He thought he was serving God zealously in persecuting the church. He was not satisfied just to see people hurt; he asked the high priest for letters to Damascus to the synagogues that if he found any there who were of the Way, whether men or women, he might bring them bound to Jerusalem (Acts 9.1-2). He believed that in this way he could serve God with fervor. But was he right? His wish to serve God was right, but his persecuting the church as a service to God was wrong. He was wrong, yet he believed himself right—this is called obsession.

Those whom the Lord refers to in John 16.2 were also the obsessed. "They shall put you out of the synagogues: yea, the hour cometh, that whosoever killeth you shall think that he offereth service unto God." To fancy that killing the disciples of the Lord is serving God, this is obsession.

Obsession is a matter of the heart. When the obsessed does something wrong, his heart insists that he is right. If a person commits wrong and asserts he is right, he is lying. But if he commits wrong and yet affirms with his mouth and believes in his heart that he is right, he is obsessed. A liar is hard without but withered up within: the more confident outwardly the more empty inwardly he becomes. An obsessed person is hard both inside and outside, being confident both within and without; for even the conscience seems to justify it.

The situation of the obsessed is such that having done something wrong he nonetheless thinks and firmly believes the thing done to be right so that no one can tell him it is wrong. This is obsession. Further, the obsessed person imagines something which has not been, as though it actually were, and his imagination goes so far as to avow that others have definitely done it. Indeed, the more he dwells on it the more certain it becomes to him. This, too, is obsession. Sometimes Christians admire a certain thing and secretly long to attain to it. At first they feel somewhat uneasy about their wish, but as they keep on thinking in that direction they gradually and increasingly are convinced of the correctness and realness of this thing. They finally take it as a truth and propagate it as truth. This also is obsession. When people are so obsessed, it is rather difficult for them to be convicted of their error, even if somebody should show them from the Word of God. This is because they can conscientiously (that is, according to conscience) say that they are right.

Hence let us be doubly careful lest we should have the slightest intention of deceiving others. We must correct inaccurate words spoken unawares. Should we utter inaccurate words with the thought of deceiving other people, we will end up deceiving ourselves.

A story was told about a brother who longed to be a zealous Christian. He thought that the voice he naturally used in prayer was not ardent enough; consequently he manufactured another voice. When he first prayed with this new voice he felt somewhat embarrassed, because it was not his own voice. But gradually he forgot what his natural voice was. People all sensed the unnaturalness of his new voice, but he took it as being natural. To deem what is unnatural to be natural is an obsession. When he first pretended, he was still conscious of its unnaturalness. But after he was obsessed, he lost his inward consciousness and accepted it as real. How very much to be pitied obsession is.

OBSESSION ILLUSTRATED IN MALACHI

One book in the Old Testament especially shows us what sort of person is the obsessed. That book is Malachi.

"I have loved you, saith Jehovah" (1.2). This is a fact. But Israel says: "Wherein hast thou loved us?" This is obsession. What they say is not the same as a common lie. They dare to say to God, "Wherein hast thou loved us?" It proves their hearts actually do not believe God has loved them. They do not believe the fact, instead they take a lie for truth. If this is not obsession, what is it?

"A son honoreth his father, and a servant his master: if then I am a father, where is mine honor? and if I am a master, where is my fear? saith Jehovah of hosts unto you, O priests, that despise my name" (1.6). This word is spoken by God. But they reply, "Wherein have we despised thy name?" They have not honored Jehovah, yet they believe they have not despised His name. This is obsession.

"Ye offer polluted bread upon mine altar" (1.7). This is God's word. Yet they come back with, "Wherein have we polluted thee?" They are wrong but they believe themselves right. This is obsession.

"And this again ye do: ye cover the altar of Jehovah with tears, with weeping, and with sighing, insomuch that he regardeth not the offering any more, neither receiveth it with good will at your hands ... Because Jehovah hath been witness between thee and the wife of thy youth, against whom thou hast dealt treacherously, though she is thy companion, and the wife of thy covenant" (2.13-14). This is fact. To it they retort, "Wherefore?" They do not believe they have done wrong. This is obsession.

"Ye have wearied Jehovah with your words" (2.17). This is fact. But they say, "Wherein have we wearied him?" Evidently they have wearied God; even so, they believe they have not. This is obsession.

"From the days of your fathers ye have turned aside from mine ordinances, and have not kept them. Return unto me, and I will return unto you, saith Jehovah of hosts" (3.7). This is what God said. But they inquired instead, "Wherein shall we return?" To themselves they are a people who have never turned aside from God's ordinances, therefore they believe there is nowhere for them to turn. This is unquestionably a case of obsession.

"Will a man rob God? Yet ye rob me" (3.8), so says God. Their answer is, "Wherein have we robbed thee?" They had robbed God in tithes and offerings, nevertheless they believed they had never robbed God. This is obsession.

"Your words have been stout against me, saith Jehovah" (3.13). This is fact. But their reply is, "What have we spoken against thee?" They have offended, yet they do not believe that they have ever offended God. This certainly is obsession.

OBSESSION ILLUSTRATED IN JOHN

There is also a book in the New Testament which touches a great deal upon obsession. It is the Gospel according to John.

"I am come in my Father's name, and ye receive me not: if another shall come in his own name, him ye will receive" (5.43). The Jews seemed to have a conscience without offence in thus rejecting the Lord Jesus. This was because of their being obsessed.

"How can ye believe, who receive glory one of another, and the glory that cometh from the only God ye seek not?" (5.44) Why did they seek that which was not glory instead of the true glory? Because they were obsessed.

"Did not Moses give you the law, and yet none of you

doeth the law? Why seek ye to kill me?" (7.19). This was what
the Lord said. But the multitude answered, "Thou hast a
demon: who seeketh to kill thee?" (v.20) They lied to the
degree of obsession, or else how could they accuse the Lord as
having a demon? They intended to kill the Lord Jesus and yet
were so obsessed as to imagine the Lord having a demon.

"Howbeit we know this man whence he is: but when the
Christ cometh, no one knoweth whence he is" (7.27). This too
was lying to the extent of being obsessed.

THE PHENOMENA OF OBSESSION

To be obsessed is most saddening and tragic. The obsessed
person falls into a most abnormal state. Let us illustrate as
follows. Some Christians are obsessed in their speech. Having
said things, they are able to believe that they have never said
them; or not having said things, they nonetheless believe that
they have said them. Things which others have never said, they
imagine and insist that they did. Such believers not only have
lied but are obsessed as well. In fact, there are some Christians
who are obsessed to such a degree that they take a lie as the
truth, wrong as right, and falsehood as fact.

Such Christians commence by thinking of deceiving others
but end up deceiving themselves. A person may lie and deceive
one, five, or even ten brothers. These brothers doubtless incur
loss, but the price the one who lies pays is exceedingly high,
for his darkness will lead him into obsession. He lies till it
becomes a habit to him. Eventually he will believe his lie to be
truth. Lying begins with deceiving others; it concludes with
obsessing one's own self. In the beginning one may still feel
somewhat uneasy, judging that it is not right for a Christian to

tell a lie. But later on, the more he lies the less he senses any wrong. In fact, the more he tells lies the more convincing he becomes; yea, he himself also believes it to be true. This is obsession. He begins with creating an unnecessary excuse to deceive others, yet ends up with himself believing it to be a fact. This is actually obsession.

Some Christians are obsessed in their testimony. After having heard the testimonies of many brothers as to how their prayers are answered, their works blessed, and their problems solved, a brother begins to dream that his prayers are answered too, his works are also blessed, and his problems are likewise solved. These, however, are not facts but mere fancies. Even so, when there is opportunity he rises up to give his testimony. He speaks so livingly that he makes what is most ordinary sound as though it were something extremely wonderful. After giving his testimony several times he actually believes it to be so. He can no longer distinguish what part is true and what part is false. He has deceived himself into believing all is true. This is obsession.

Some believers are obsessed in sickness. Their physical bodies are actually healthy, yet they assume they have certain sicknesses. Many of their illnesses arise from self-love. They are not sick; for the doctors cannot diagnose any ailment; but because they love themselves so much they complain of this or that discomfort. If their hearts beat but just a little faster, they conclude that they must have heart trouble. If they cough slightly a bit more, they are sure they have tuberculosis. Should the doctors tell them the truth that they are not at all sick, they retort with how incompetent those doctors are. But should the doctors go along with them and say they are sick indeed, they praise their doctors again and again as being highly skillful. Not having an illness yet insisting that one has—this is obsession. It is the result of self-love. It may well begin with the hidden desire to obtain sympathy from his family, friends, or relatives, but it eventually concludes with the person truly believing himself to be ill. He creates his sickness through psychology. This is obsession, for obsession is creating something by which to deceive one's own self till one is no longer conscious of being deceived.

Some of God's people are obsessed with fear. One may harbor a fear in his heart without anything terribly having happened. In the beginning it may simply be a thought that a certain thing is terrible. But then, the real fear descends upon him. You may tell him many reasons why it is not terrifying; still, you will not be able to convince him. No matter who tells him the truth, he believes in the falsehood. This too is obsession.

Some Christians are obsessed by their conjectures. Due to the lack of light such believers frequently take conjectures as facts. At first one may only guess that the other person has done a certain thing or uttered certain words or frequented a certain place; subsequently, though, he believes that the person in question has actually done that thing or spoken that word or frequented that place. He is so obsessed that he imagines the thing which has never occurred. His accusation is clearly unjustified; nevertheless he believes it to be true. This is obsession. He believes what is not true of other people. This is obsession. He takes conjecture as fact. This is obsession.

There is another kind of obsession. Some saints are truly seeking the Lord. They expect to walk perfectly before Him. Yet they do not have light. Such a person may look upon himself as having done something wrong when there was nothing at all wrong. He worries himself to death about it. He even goes to the extreme of sighing that the Lord cannot forgive him nor can the precious blood cleanse him from this sin. Judging by the light of God we can only conclude that he has not at all sinned. But he avows that he *has* sinned, that he has committed a terrible transgression. He agonizes; he sheds many tears. He confesses it not one time but hundreds of times. He confesses all the time because he feels his sin is always present with him. What do you call this? This too is obsession. One is not necessarily obsessed in bad things; there is the possibility of being obsessed even by the conviction of sin. A seeking Christian may condemn himself unnecessarily if he lacks light. To believe what is not a fact—this is obsession.

"Woe unto them that call evil good, and good evil; that put darkness for light, and light for darkness; that put bitter for sweet, and sweet for bitter!" (Is. 5.20) One may be so obsessed as to call evil good and good evil, to put darkness for light and light for darkness, and to take bitter for sweet and sweet for bitter. He is plainly wrong, yet he is confident of being right. How much to be pitied is this condition! What a Christian ought to be most afraid of is having sin and yet not seeing that sin. Having sin is a question of defilement, but not seeing sin is a matter of darkness. Defilement is dangerous enough; adding darkness to defilement is doubly dangerous. A Christian who lives in darkness cannot easily walk in the path which lies before him because he does not see the way.

The phenomena of obsession are many and varied. A believer has the possibility of being obsessed in his thought regarding himself or others, in his words concerning himself or others, in his spiritual situation, in his sins, and in everything in relation to himself. Obsession is actually a very common symptom. Each and every Christian may be obsessed; the difference lies only in the degree. Hence we cannot but take note of it.

chapter 5

obsession: causes and deliverance

For every obsession there is a cause. We will try to find out some of the basic causes by looking closely through the Scriptures.

LOVE DARKNESS

People love darkness rather than light. This is a main cause for obsession. Such abnormal love reveals the straying of the heart, hence such ones are easily obsessed. In order to avoid difficulties and to save themselves from troubles, they dare not face the light but try to comfort themselves that they are right. Gradually they really believe they are right. Thus are they obsessed. The Jews rejected the Lord Jesus because they loved darkness rather than light (John 3.19). They had no light for they dwelt in darkness. They imagined that it was reasonable for them to hate and to reject the Lord Jesus. "If I had not done among them the works which none other did," said the Lord, "they had not had sin: but now have they both seen and hated both me and my Father" (John 15.24). Why? Because they were obsessed. They hated the Lord without a cause. We need to know that wherever there is darkness and no light, there are erroneous concepts, false confidence, and wrong judgment. There is an element of obsession in each and every error. The consequence of not loving the light is obsession.

PRIDE

Pride is also a major reason for obsession. "The pride of thy heart hath deceived thee" (Obadiah 3). This reveals that the greatest reason for self-deception is pride. Those who deceive themselves into obsession are probably all proud people. If a Christian sets his heart on vainglory and position before men, he may start to pretend to be what he is not in order to deceive people. Gradually he begins to deceive himself and to become obsessed. Once he becomes proud he can easily imagine himself as having something extraordinary. Slowly he will take what he fancies as the truth. Thus he falls into obsession. Brothers and sisters, never consider pride to be an insignificant sin, for pride can easily propel us into obsession. Let us therefore learn to be humble.

RECEIVE NOT THE LOVE OF THE TRUTH

Not receiving the love of the truth is another big cause behind obsession. It is shown in 2 Thessalonians that for those who "received not the love of the truth . . . God sendeth them a working of error, that they should believe a lie" (2.10-11). This is indeed a most terrible aftermath. People are obsessed by believing lies. They believe things which are non-existent. Because of their not receiving the love of truth, they just naturally incline towards lies.

"Buy the truth, and sell it not, yea, wisdom, and instruction, and understanding" (Prov. 23.23). Truth needs to be bought, that is, a price must be paid. Blessed are we if our hearts are well prepared for the truth of God. We will love the truth and accept it whatever it may cost us. But oftentimes men do not have the love of the truth in them. They distort the truth and even discard it. Finally they actually believe it is not the truth. They proclaim as untrue what is the truth and preach as the truth what is untrue. They seem to do this with confidence. This definitely is obsession.

We ought to know that once a person rejects the love of the truth in his heart, it is very difficult for him to see that truth later on. There was once a brother who studied in a theological seminary. He went to talk with one of his professors about the matter of baptism. Said this brother, "I have seen before God that I was crucified with the Lord. I am already dead; I need to be buried; I should be baptized. What do you think of it?" That professor answered: "Once before I too had a similar experience. Just before I was to graduate from the seminary, as you do now I also saw this matter of co-death, co-burial and co-resurrection. I saw that I had already died, that I should be buried in baptism. But if I were to be baptized by immersion, I could not work in the denomination to which I belonged. I prayed about it and felt that I could postpone the decision till after graduation and ordination. I graduated from the seminary and was ordained a pastor. And now it has been many years since. Though I have not been baptized, I have got along quite well. So, why don't you concentrate on your study? After your graduation and ordination, this problem may not trouble you at all." To live peacefully after breaching the truth—this is none other than obsession. Fortunately, that brother did not listen to his professor. Brothers and sisters, remember that we may easily be obsessed if our heart is not absolute towards God.

SEEK NOT THE GLORY
THAT COMES FROM THE ONLY GOD

Not seeking the glory which comes from the only God is also a factor in obsession. "How can ye believe, who receive glory one of another, and the glory that cometh from the only God ye seek not?" asks the Lord Jesus (John 5.44). For the sake of coveting glory from men the Jews rejected the Lord and lost eternal life. How very lamentable! This inordinate love of glory from men inclined their hearts to a lie. As a consequence, they believed in falsehood. They became increasingly confident of themselves. They were none other than obsessed.

THE DELIVERANCE: SEE LIGHT IN GOD'S LIGHT

Obsession is tragic. The children of God should not be obsessed. The obsessed cannot see the true character of things. Thus, in the words which follow we will briefly point out how to see reality and how to avoid confusion.

> *Who is among you that feareth Jehovah, that*
> *obeyeth the voice of his servant? he that walketh*

> *in darkness, and hath no light, let him trust in the*
> *name of Jehovah, and rely upon his God. Behold,*
> *all ye that kindle a fire, that gird yourselves about*
> *with firebrands; walk ye in the flame of your fire,*
> *and among the brands that ye have kindled. This*
> *shall ye have of my hand; ye shall lie down in*
> *sorrow. (Is. 50.10-11).*

When the Israelites walked in darkness and had no light, they most naturally kindled many firebrands with which to surround themselves. They would walk in the flame of their own fire. Was this good? Not at all, for the consequence was that they lay down in sorrows. Spiritual darkness cannot be dispelled by man-made firebrands. The light must come from God, not from man. Human torches can never enable people to see spiritual reality.

Let us accordingly understand that the firebrand which we ourselves kindle can never be a source of spiritual light. Some Christians say: "Where can I be wrong! I do not think I have done anything amiss. I do not feel I am at all wrong." Are you really that dependable? Others may say: "I have deliberated long on this particular matter. I dare to conclude that it is definitely right." Is it correct to assume that because you have deliberated, you can therefore definitely decide? According to the Word of God, this is not the way for Christians to know a thing. You may exhaust your mental power in deliberating, but all which will be ignited out of that will be your human torch. A Christian cannot walk along his spiritual path by the light of his own firebrand. He must depend on the name of the Lord. Only by trusting in God can he really see and so walk spiritually. We frequently become more confused by our much thinking, we may even be deceived. Spiritual light does not come from our feeling or thought. The more one seeks for light within himself the less light he has, for the light is not in him.

"For with thee is the fountain of life: In thy light shall we see light" (Ps. 36.9). It is only by the light of God that we truly see light, that is, see the true character of a thing. The first light is that which enlightens, the second light is the true character which is seen. We need to live in the light of God if we wish to see the true character of a matter.

Brothers and sisters, it is a big problem how we live. If we live in the light of God's life we can be a people who see. There are some Christians for whom we have great respect not only for their intrinsic goodness but also for their living before God. "God is light" (1 John 1.5). All who know God know light. All who know light are found to have God in them. A person who knows the light of God is able, as soon as he meets you, to discern your true character and to point out your faults. It is not that he is trying to pick on you but it is entirely due to the sharpness of his inward eye. With the one who does not have light, he may think that a certain thing is pretty good; however, it must be left to the one who lives in the light of God to discover the true character of the thing. No flashlight is necessary under the bright sunshine; no human firebrand is needed under God's light. If we were to live in the light of God, the true character of a thing would be as clear and transparent as light.

Those who know themselves in the light of God know their own selves indeed. If we are not in God's light we may sin without being conscious of how wicked our sin is, we may fall without being fully aware of how shameful our fall is. We may do a little good outwardly but how deceitful is our inward state. We may show gentleness outside, but who knows how hard we are inside. We may put on a spiritual form, but in our reality we are full of the flesh. When the light of God comes, the true character of all these things shall be manifested. We will then see through ourselves; we will confess how blind we were before!

Herein is the difference between the Old and the New Testaments: in the Old Testament, people know right and wrong by outward law; in the New Testament, we know the true character of a thing by the indwelling Holy Spirit. It is possible that we see our fault through doctrine or teaching, but even so we have yet to see our fault in the light of God. Knowing our fault through doctrine or teaching is superficial; perceiving our fault in God's light alone is thorough. Only in the light of God can we see what God sees. This is the meaning of seeing light in God's light.

If we do not want to be obsessed we must live in the light of God. Our greatest temptation is to kindle our own firebrand. Whenever we are confronted with a problem, immediately we try to search out the answer ourselves. We ourselves attempt to decide what is right and what is wrong. Brothers and sisters, this is not the way God wants us to go. We need to be humble, acknowledging how unreliable we are. Our judgment is undependable, our thought is undependable, our action is undependable. We are subject to error. What we judge as right may not necessarily be right; what we judge as wrong may not be wrong at all. That which we consider to be sweet may actually be bitter, and vice versa. That which we take as light may not be light after all, and that which we take as darkness may turn out not to be darkness. We must not substitute for the light of God the firebrands which we ourselves kindle. We should receive light from God.

"The lamp of the body is the eye: if therefore thine eye be single, thy whole body shall be full of light. But if thine eye be

evil, thy whole body shall be full of darkness. If therefore the
light that is in thee be darkness, how great is the darkness!"
(Matt. 6.22-23) A Christian who has no light in him tends to
be obsessed. What a pity if one does not see what he ought to
see and does not know what he ought to know. We must ask
God to shine through us that we may touch Him. A Christian
life should not be filled with problems, doubts and hesitations.
We ought to be able to see whether it be right or wrong. If we
can see, we will avoid being obsessed.

"If any man willeth to do his will, he shall know of the
teaching, whether it be of God, or whether I speak from
myself" (John 7.17). The condition for enlightenment is that
we genuinely want the will of God. Let us not hastily and
confidently decide any matter which comes before us. Rather
let us ask God to give us a perfect heart to do the will of God.
A hardened heart, a selfish heart, a self-reliant heart may shut
out God's light. If we wish to have the light of God we must
be tender, unselfish, and not self-reliant. In short, we must be
humble. May we ask God to deliver us, that daily we may live
in His light and thus be able to know what is trueness and
reality. May God save us from falsehood and obsession.